The Library of Writing Skills™

A Step-by-Step Guide to
Persuasive
Writing

Lauren Spencer

The Rosen Publishing Group, Inc., New York

To all those opinionated folks who are not afraid to express their thoughts

Published in 2005 by The Rosen Publishing Group, Inc.
29 East 21st Street, New York, NY 10010

Library of Congress Cataloging-in-Publication Data

Spencer, Lauren.
A step-by-step guide to persuasive writing / Lauren Spencer—1st ed.
   p. cm. — (The library of writing skills)
Includes bibliographical references and index.
ISBN 1-4042-0217-X (library binding)
ISBN 1-4042-5309-2 (pbk.)
6-pack ISBN 1-4042-5315-7
1. English language—Rhetoric. 2. Persuasion (Rhetoric) 3. Report writing.
I. Title. II. Series: Spencer, Lauren, Library of writing skills.
PE1431.S6 2005
                                                                2004002690

Manufactured in the United States of America

Table of Contents

Introduction

Persuasive writing introduces an author's strong opinions regarding a specific subject he or she has chosen to write about. When you are writing persuasively about something, your goal is to convince the reader that your opinion is relevant. You do this by using language that conveys balanced thoughts, strong convictions, and respect for the reader.

Persuasive pieces often use emotional subject matter that is based on a personal opinion, such as a letter written to another person describing something you feel strongly about. Reviews are also a form of persuasive writing. They are meant to convince a reader whether it is a good idea to experience whatever is being reviewed. Writing that argues a specific point can often be found on the editorial page of a newspaper. This type of writing generally focuses on topics for which there are many different opinions and possible arguments.

When writing persuasively, it is crucial that your thoughts are explained clearly and that your opinions are supported by facts. In some cases, detailed research will be required to fully support your opinions. In other cases, your writing will rely more on your own personal beliefs. Since persuasive writing cannot exist without an audience, respect for the reader is an absolute requirement.

In this book, we will explore various methods for focusing on, investigating, organizing, and writing about a topic so that you can explain your opinions in a convincing manner. We will investigate ways to involve the audience and make your writing more exciting by using figurative language such as similes, metaphors, hyperbole, and personification. Anecdotes and rhetorical questions are other devices that make persuasive pieces more expressive. We will find ways to define opinions with passion and style, which are two important elements of any persuasive writing piece.

1

Prewriting

When you are writing persuasively, your aim is to convince the reader of your point of view. By expressing your opinion, which is based on feelings but supported by facts, your audience reads your interpretation of a specific subject or event. The difference between writing subjectively (when you express only feelings) and objectively (when you present only facts) is the difference between persuasive and informative writing. In informative writing, the author generally avoids expressing strong feelings. In persuasive pieces, the author's feelings take center stage. These feelings and opinions, when supported by research, are used to influence a reader's attitude toward the subject.

As you are conveying your opinions, keep your audience in mind. Although you want to convince people of your point of view, you do not want them to feel as if you're lecturing them or telling them how to feel. Let readers "see" your point of view, and then they can make up their own minds. In

KEY

✔ **Read and understand different persuasive writing styles such as the newspaper's editorial section, or a book or movie review.**

✔ **Choose a persuasive topic.**

✔ **Explore powers of opinion.**

doing so, you avoid talking down to your audience while encouraging them to think for themselves.

Persuasive pieces can be written in a few different formats. You may choose to write a persuasive letter to someone about your opinion on a specific topic. Reviews are also a form of persuasive writing. These short pieces express your feelings about something specific, such as a book or movie. Your aim is to convince readers whether they should try it. You can review anything: art, literature, food, or any subject in between.

Writing that takes a specific side on an issue where there may be existing disagreement or controversy is known as an argument piece. Although an argument piece may involve a less personal topic than a persuasive essay, it needs to be just as strong-willed. In an argument piece, you need to recognize the opposing view while supporting your opinion with facts.

Point of View

Persuasive writing is usually written in the first person, which means a first-person pronoun such as I is used throughout the piece. Persuasive writing is also often written in the present tense. This allows the reader to become involved in the topic, seeing the issue through the author's eyes. If you feel strongly about your subject, your beliefs will come through in the writing.

As you think about possible topics, always keep your reader in mind. Make sure you can communicate to this

ASK YOURSELF

- ☐ Have I chosen a format to fit my topic?

- ☐ Do I feel strongly enough about my topic?

- ☐ Have I listed all the pros and cons of my topic?

person the importance of your subject. You want the audience to have every reason to believe as strongly as you do in the topic. Address the reader as "you," and treat him or her the way you would a friend with whom you want to share valuable information. By using a confident tone in your writing, which is your personality and author's "voice," you'll convey how strongly you believe in your cause. It takes logic, organization, and patience, but eventually your point will be clear enough for your reader to decide whether he or she has been persuaded.

Choosing a Topic

Since it's crucial that you care about the topic you choose, take some time to reflect on your options. On a blank sheet of paper, make a list of things that you feel strongly about. The list can include topics such as "Schools should offer computers with Internet access in every classroom" or something on a larger scale that you've thought about for a while, such as "Educators should not have the authority to search students' lockers."

An easy way to get all your ideas on paper is to choose a few topics about different aspects of your life. Think of issues you deal with at home, at school, and while you're with friends. Once you've written down several ideas, return to each topic and list the reasons why you feel strongly about each statement. When you find a subject that you have many opinions about, it's a safe bet this could become your topic. If you have a couple of choices, ask other people's views on each statement. Their answers may help you to form a stronger opinion.

In order to firm up your opinions on any topic, put together a graphic organizer called a pro-and-con list. Example:

Computers with Internet access in every classroom	
PROS	**CONS**
Students can do more research in class.	Students might be distracted from class work.
Teachers can use examples from the Internet.	Students might argue about when they get to use the computer.
Interactive projects can be done right in the classroom.	Students might visit inappropriate Web sites.

When constructing your pro-and-con list, take the reasons from your list and make them the examples that appear in each column, either supporting (pro) or arguing against (con) your topic. Your reader will appreciate that both sides of the topic are presented. This will show you've taken the time to look at the issue from different viewpoints. This is why writing a pro-and-con list will expand your opinion and improve your piece.

Exercise: Write It Out

Think of a past vacation or day trip that was a disaster and write two paragraphs about it. The first paragraph must be completely factual. Use the

Opinions Vs. Facts

An opinion is a belief about something that is neither true nor false because it is a personal and subjective feeling. Facts, on the other hand, are details that can be proved. Facts refer to things that actually exist or have happened; therefore, they can be proved true. For example, the statement "There is one computer in the classroom" is a fact, while the statement "The computer isn't any good" is an opinion.

five *Ws*: **Who** went? **Where** did you travel? **When** did you go? **Why** did you go? Consider only facts, such as "Mom and Dad both had time off from work and I didn't have school." **What** happened? Again, write only about facts, such as "We boarded an airplane for a twelve-hour flight."

In the second paragraph, write your personal opinions to describe how you felt about the experience. Use descriptive details to describe your feelings surrounding the trip and what happened during your stay. When you are finished writing, reread both paragraphs. Which one do you like best? Which one has more personality?

Evaluating Your Opinion Statement

After you have formed an opinion statement and made a pro-and-con list, the time has come to think logically about your viewpoint. It is now time to judge, evaluate, and prove your opinion statement with relevant facts.

This factual information can be gleaned by doing research related to your topic. Be careful, however. If you have chosen an opinion that is too general such as "All Internet access in schools is useful," then you might have difficulty proving your point. Avoid using words in your opinion statement that are too strongly aligned with or opposed to any argument. Words that are commonly too positive or too negative to use as part of an opinion statement include *all*, *every*, *never*, *none*, *best*, and *worst*. If your opinion statement uses any of these words, it might be impossible to support with fact-based research.

Research and Organization

Before you gather the factual information you'll use to support your opinion statement, decide how you want to organize your topic. Because you are presenting how you feel about a specific subject, arrange your points in the order you feel they are most effective. By prioritizing your facts and ideas, you'll be able to take your reader through your thought process in stages. If you build your opinion gradually, the reader will be able to gain a clear and thorough understanding of your opinion. Sometimes writers begin with their least important points and build arguments that are more convincing later. In other cases, this order can be reversed. Writers may begin by starting the piece with their most important and dramatic evidence and following with supporting fact.

Think of at least three points that will support your opinion. These ideas will serve as the foundation for your outline. If your persuasive topic is "Hip-hop music is here

KEY

✔ **Organize your thoughts.**

✔ **Outline your idea.**

✔ **Research facts to support your opinion.**

to stay," your three supporting points might be hip-hop is popular; hip-hop is the voice of a generation; and hip-hop is the future of popular music. Writing your persuasive piece in this direction is a little like a fireworks display: It begins with a bang and then builds to a great crescendo.

Next, you need to create an outline. There are two types of outlines. A topic outline is organized with a list of words or phrases. This type of outline is most often used for shorter essays. A sentence outline organizes the ideas in complete thoughts, so more information can be included. Longer reports and research papers usually require sentence outlines. With either type of outline, you want to make sure that you include enough information so that you can pick up the thought and expand on it. Be very specific in your outline by focusing on one thought at a time. Example:

Topic Outline
Topic: Hip-hop music is here to stay.

    I.   Popular
- CD and concert sales high
- People watch videos/copy hip-hop styles
- Hip-hop influences other art forms

    II. Voice of a generation
- Authentic performers
- Performers can relate to audience
- Respect for audience

III. Future of popular music

- Emerging artists
- Critical praise
- Hip-hop music evolves

Sentence Outline
Topic: Hip-hop music is here to stay.

I.   Hip-hop is very popular.

- Hip-hop CD and concert sales are higher than most other styles of music.
- Hip-hop artists often start fashion trends.
- Hip-hop style and fashion have influenced other art forms, such as movies.

II.   Hip-hop is the voice of a generation.

- Hip-hop performers are authentic in their words and dress.
- Hip-hop performers can relate to their audience.
- Hip-hop artists respect their audience based on their lyrics.

III. The future of hip-hop is strong.

- New hip-hop artists are constantly emerging.
- Hip-hop artists have received continuous critical praise.
- Hip-hop music is constantly changing to include new sounds and trends.

Supporting Your Opinion

A well-written persuasive piece requires factual support. By doing adequate research on your subject, you can find factual information such as statistics, sales records, charts, and graphs and combine that data with other people's critical opinions. Sometimes when you find an opposing viewpoint, you can use it to strengthen your idea by explaining why you *don't* agree. Whenever you take this approach, stay focused on why you feel strongly about your viewpoint. Avoid criticizing the other person's opinion or being disrespectful in your writing.

To find factual details, reference books such as encyclopedias contain information you can use to support your subject. For instance, if you need to find the date that the term "hip-hop" was first used, an online encyclopedia dealing with current music will have that data. Magazines, newspapers, and Web sites often supply information that includes more opinion-based material. These sources can be invaluable since your persuasive piece will be stronger if you can cite someone else backing up your opinion. Citing a critical opinion, or one given by a person who is respected as an authority in a related field, is also useful if you need to prove a point by argument. If you use any of the information word-for-word from one of your

ASK YOURSELF

☐ Is my information clearly organized?

☐ Are there enough facts to support my opinion or do I need to conduct additional research?

☐ Have I recorded my sources accurately?

research sources, you must also include the name of that source in your piece. This way you won't be accused of plagiarism, which is a very serious charge. Example:

In the November 2002 issue of *The Source* magazine, editor in chief David Mays said, "Hip-hop is the voice of a generation."

It's important that what David Mays actually said is surrounded by quotation marks and that you also credit the magazine where you found the quote. You can also paraphrase a comment, which means you give credit to the source while rearranging the words so that you don't need to use quote marks. Example:

When David Mays mentioned in the November 2002 issue of *The Source* magazine that he thought hip-hop was the voice of a generation, I thought he made a great point.

Using Your Sources

The key to a successful persuasive piece is the ability to gain access to a variety of facts and opinions and to use them effectively. This means using the information from your outline to give you the direction to find facts or ideas to include in your writing. As you locate various facts and opinions, write them down. You can do this on the outline itself (see example) or by creating a reference chart. For a chart, make two columns on the page. In the first column, copy all the points from your outline. In the second column, note where you found those facts and opinions. If at certain times during your writing you need to refresh your memory or find a similar fact, you can look to your chart for your original source.

Outline Facts	Sources
CD sales high	*New York Times*, April 15, 2004
Concerts sell out	*New York Times*, April 15, 2004
People watch videos/copy style	*The Source* magazine, January 2001
Performers authentic	*Vibe* magazine, November 2004
Performers can relate	*Vibe* magazine, November 2004
Respect for community	Youth in Action, online site
New artists	*The Source* magazine, January 2001
Critics wrong	*New York Times*, January 12, 1999
Changes in sound	*Rolling Stone* magazine, September 13, 2003

Organizing your sources before you begin writing is helpful because it allows you to focus primarily on writing about your opinions, the true nature of persuasive writing. The purpose of your research is to effectively support your views on the topic.

If you are writing a review, be sure that you have your sources handy, whether that is the book you read, CD you listened to, or the notes you took during the event. With all this information to back you up, you can let your opinions loose on the page in an organized and convincing manner.

3

Writing Your First Draft

As we have learned, the main objective of persuasive writing is to convince your reader of your opinion. While you're expecting your readers to make their own decisions about the subject, your goal is to help them see things your way. To do this, you need to be confident of your author's voice, or the tone and style of your writing. Your author's voice is meant to appeal to, interest, and persuade your reader. Quite often teachers will say, "Write like you speak," and while that is often true in persuasive writing, you want to make sure you use language that is clear. This will make it easier for your reader to see your point of view.

If you are a person who likes to present his or her opinions in a formal way, that style will come through in your piece. If a conversational style is more to your liking, focus your writing in that way. Never insult your reader or suggest that he or she would be foolish not to see the issue as you do. Persuasive writing is meant to point out a certain opinion that

KEY

✔ **Focus your point of view and zero in on your author's voice.**

✔ **Apply different writing transitions and techniques.**

✔ **Write your first draft.**

is supported by facts. Once you've presented your idea, it is up to readers to make their own decisions.

Writing Transitions

In a persuasive story, the way you present your thoughts is very important. If your sentences are not well connected, your readers will be confused. Transitional words and phrases help to ensure a smooth ride for the reader. Phrases such as "therefore," "in fact," or "for this reason" will connect your thoughts in an authoritative way. When writing to persuade, remember to include the opposing point of view in a positive light. This will show that, although you recognize the other side of the issue, your opinion still makes the most sense.

TRANSITIONAL WORDS: To Add Information			
Again	And	Besides	Finally
Along with	Another	For example	In addition
Also	As well	For instance	Next

Writing Reviews

A review, whether of a book or movie, is a special type of persuasive writing. It expresses to the reader your opinion about what you read or saw without giving any surprises away. It is also important in any type of review to mention the title of the piece and the person who created it at the beginning. Reviews of art or restaurants also require the writer to be very clear about what is being experienced. The more facts you present

ASK YOURSELF

- [ ] Does my author's voice come through clearly?

- [ ] Is my opinion strongly stated?

- [ ] Do I stick to the point?

- [ ] Did I use literary techniques to bring my first draft to life?

at the beginning, the more freedom you have to write about how you feel. This information should help persuade your reader. Don't assume that he or she has any clue about your topic. Take readers on a journey into the experience by using descriptive elements. Consider how the experience made you "see," "hear," "smell," "taste," and "touch" like never before, and use descriptive details to provoke those senses.

Adding Style

In any effective writing, the use of figurative language and other literary techniques will add style while capturing a reader's attention. Here are some examples of figures of speech that add personality to your writing:

Anecdote: A short and interesting story drawn from life that is used to make a point. Example:

> The high school talent show featured musical acts that, because of their professionalism, reminded me of the performers I saw at the *American Idol* taping.

Rhetorical Question: The word "rhetoric" means to use words effectively. A rhetorical question is one posed for effect. When posing a rhetorical question, no answer is expected. A rhetorical question involves the reader directly. Example:

Is it actually possible for a dozen high school students to make the school auditorium feel like a Broadway stage?

Emotive Language: This is when drama is used to evoke strong feelings from the reader. Example:

Imagine being surrounded by the powerful voices of the most talented students that the high school has to offer.

Hyperbole: Exaggeration adds effect to further make the point. Example:

Imagine being surrounded by the most amazing high school singing voices that the world has ever heard.

Parallel: When you point out both sides of the issue, you are using a parallel. Example:

To be swept away by talent is wonderful; to be swept out of the door by a bad performance is painful.

Figurative Language: Using similes, metaphors, and personification to bring your persuasive writing to life. Example of a simile:

When the members of the choral group sang, their voices lit up the stage like fireworks.

Example of a metaphor:

They made an explosion of sound.

Example of personification:

Their microphones practically danced across the stage.

Writing the First Draft

As you begin writing your first draft, refer to your outline and research. Make sure you have some uninterrupted time so that you can get all your thoughts on the page without stopping.

Your opening sentence or paragraph must capture the reader's attention by involving him or her in your topic. To accomplish this, address your audience directly by using "you" or "we." Also, appeal to the reader's sense of excitement by enticing him or her into the topic with an anecdote or fact. There is no need to state what is already obvious, such as "a school talent show is a big event." Begin instead with a statement about talent shows that will immediately resonate with a reader.

When presenting your point of view, be sure you are reasonable. Since persuasive writing is meant to convince the reader of something he or she may not agree with or be aware of, take your time in explaining why you feel the way you do. Although confidence is an important element in persuasive writing, avoid boasting or bragging. This approach will often turn the reader off both the subject and the writer. Support your claims with well-researched facts. The order in which you present your information often means the difference between convincing the reader or just piquing his or her interest. Writing about your topic in a systematic manner will let the reader know that you have taken the time to fully support your opinions.

The final paragraph of your persuasive piece is extremely important. This is the last chance you have in which to state your opinion. Your goal is to leave the reader with a strong sense of why he or she should consider your viewpoint. To do this, restate your original opinion in a new way. Decide for your reader exactly what you would like him or her to remember about your topic. If it makes sense and isn't too overly dramatic, end with a personal appeal, such as "I recommend strongly that you do not miss this year's high school talent show." Example:

High School Hullabaloo

This year's high school talent show was right on, not only because of the students' talent but also because of its smooth organization.

The auditorium was packed with what seemed like thousands of people. I was lucky to get a good seat. The first performer was Tracy Warner, and she moved me with a rendition of "Girls Just Want to Have Fun." It was phenomenal. Her voice shook the building like an earthquake.

After Greg Epson's group, the Crimsons, belted out four rap-metal tunes, there was a short intermission. The second half was just as excellent as the first. What impressed me the most was the composure of each performer. It reminded me of the time I watched *American Idol* being taped, and the singers acted as if they'd been performing all their lives. If you go to see only one high school production this year, make it this one. You won't be sorry!

4

Revising Your First Draft

Revision is the act of reexamining and improving your writing. Revising does not mean correcting spelling and punctuation, which will come later. Revising means to investigate your draft and make sure the ideas flow in an organized and logical manner and that the language you've used will hold the reader's interest.

With a red pen in hand—or any color that stands out on the page—start your revision by examining your writing for areas where you can cut unnecessary or repeated information. You want to avoid writing that rambles on and fails to make its point. Next, read through the piece to make sure that the order of each sentence flows and supports your main opinion. Check to ensure you've answered any questions that your reader might have about the topic and that your ideas are supported with facts. Look for loose ends and tie them up by rewriting or adding details to support your main idea. Finally, make sure that the language you are using expresses your enthusiasm for your subject. Look for places where you can express strong emotion. As you check for these elements, make changes directly on the page.

Writing for Clarity

Since your persuasive piece ultimately depends on your ability to deliver a strong opinion, you must make sure that your subject has been presented clearly. Doing this will ensure that the reader understands your message without becoming confused. As you revise your first draft, make sure that all of your opinions are supported by facts. When a statement is made that is not supported, it can confuse the reader. Here are some examples of unclear writing:

Wearing school uniforms saves lives.

This sentence jumps to a conclusion. The statement is an exaggeration since there is no proof that it is true. By adding a qualifier such as "in my opinion" at the beginning and then continuing to explain why you feel so strongly about this statement, you will impress upon the reader that this is your opinion. Example:

Students never fight over school uniforms.

This statement sets up a situation that makes school uniforms seem more powerful than they are. Soften the statement by using factual support: "In my research, I've found that students almost never fight over school uniforms, whereas without uniforms . . ." Example:

In schools where there are no uniforms, fights break out every day.

This sentence contains an exaggerated half-truth. By showing that there is less fighting in schools where uniforms are required, the point would be delivered in a more convincing way: "Last year, Morris High School had twice as many fights over clothing worn at the school than Bellmore, where the students wear uniforms." Example:

School uniforms are perfect because everyone likes them.

This sentence suggests that because "everyone" likes school uniforms, they are good. Just because many people like something doesn't necessarily mean it's a good thing. If you want to make a similar point, take a poll or do a study of some sort and use the results for your piece: "Sixty-eight percent of those students asked said that they thought school uniforms eliminated some tensions between students. It seems that more people like them than not." Example:

School uniforms are like the outfits astronauts wear in space.

This statement is incomplete because it compares two things that are not similar. If the sentence is used as a comparison, you must back it up with a reason: "School uniforms are like the outfits astronauts wear in outer space because students are also constantly exploring new territory."

ASK YOURSELF

☐ Do your ideas and thoughts flow smoothly?

☐ Is your persuasive point supported clearly?

☐ Are your sentences varied enough to make them interesting?

Sentence Structure

Because you don't want the reader to be distracted from your persuasive opinion by choppy or otherwise poor sentence structure, make sure your piece includes complete, informative sentences. The types of sentences that will make your opinion felt most strongly are declarative, imperative, and exclamatory. Also, a mix of complex and compound sentences will give your writing more variety. Example: Here is a letter written to persuade the school superintendent about why school uniforms are worthwhile.

November 7, 2004

14 Somewhere Rd.

Thistown, Somestate 55535

Ms. Cecelia Superior

Superintendent of Schools

Thistown, Somestate 55535

Dear Ms. Superior:

During lunch with my classmates the other day,
the subject turned to school uniforms. My name is
Sally Clipper and I attend Bellmore High School.
It is an excellent school, and it has gotten even better
in the last two years since we've had mandatory school
uniforms. Before students wore uniforms, there were
always fights over someone taking someone else's jacket
or hat. There was a lot of attitude from one student to
another about who was wearing the latest "fashions" and
who was cool or not based on what he or she was wearing.
Because our school doesn't have these problems anymore,
we can now focus on educating our minds.

When I read in our local paper that you were
thinking of reversing the uniform policy in our school,
I decided I had to write and let you know how I
feel. I also thought it would be helpful if I took a
student poll so you could see how others felt about this
decision. On Tuesday of last week, I asked students,
teachers, and parents about school uniforms. This is
what I found out: 73 percent felt that uniforms were a
good thing; 17 percent wanted to go back to a "no-
uniform" policy, and 10 percent had no opinion.

As you can see, a majority of our school community
prefers school uniforms. When I asked for their reasons,
the answers ranged from "because it makes it easier to

Types of Sentences

Declarative Sentence: A declarative sentence makes a statement about a person, place, thing, or idea. Example:

> *The colors of our school uniforms are blue-and-yellow-checked skirts for the girls, blue pants for the boys, and white shirts for everybody.*

Imperative Sentence: The point of an imperative sentence is to give a command. It is aimed directly at the reader. Example:

> *Consider all the money saved on clothes when students wear uniforms to school instead of traditional clothing.*

Exclamatory Sentence: A strong emotion or surprise is expressed in an exclamatory sentence and is usually followed by an explanation point. Example:

> *It would be great to never have to worry about what to wear!*

Complex Sentence: When you put a dependent clause—so-called because it can't exist alone—into a complete sentence, it makes a complex sentence. Example:

> *The student uniforms, which include our school colors, look great during athletic events and pep rallies.*

While the sentence "The student uniforms look great during athletic events and pep rallies" is complete on its own, adding the dependent clause "which include our school colors" adds a detail that gives the reader more information.

Compound Sentence: Taking two complete sentences—sentences that have a subject and a verb and can stand on their own—and joining them together creates a compound sentence. You can accomplish this by using a semicolon or conjunction, which is a word used to join sentence elements. Words like "and," "or," and "but" are conjunctions. Examples:

> *School uniforms look crisp and neat on the first day of class; you have to clean them every day in order for them to stay that way.*

Or you can use a conjunction:

> *School uniforms look crisp and neat on the first day of class, but you have to clean them every day in order for them to stay that way.*

get dressed in the morning" to "I never get grief from anyone about what I wear."

Based on these results, I ask you, Ms. Superior, would you rather have a calm and clean student body focused on learning, or a disorderly mass of students distracted by fashion trends? Please reconsider your decision to reverse the uniform policy at Bellmore High!

Yours truly,

Sally Clipper

Now that you have begun the revision process and have checked your writing for its sentence structure and overall clarity, it is also a good time to examine its ratio of facts to opinions. Make sure that each

Trade Off

Since a persuasive piece is one that contains emotion, it is a good idea to read it aloud to check if the powers of persuasion really work. A great way to find this out is to switch your paper with a partner and have him or her read it to you. Are you convinced? Make a copy for yourself so that you can keep notes about where you can make useful changes.

strong opinion is supported by one or more factual statements, and that your research has been properly cited throughout your work. You can always refer to your source chart if you neglected to include this information earlier. In addition, examine your writing line by line to search for awkward phrasing, incomplete or unclear thoughts, or arguments that seem illogical. We will revise and edit your draft further in the following chapter.

Writing a Letter

After getting permission from a principal or teacher, choose someone in the public eye—such as a celebrity, politician, or athlete—and write a persuasive letter to that person explaining all the reasons he or she should come to your school to speak to students during career day.

Proofreading and Editing

When you are writing to persuade your reader, your title will need to reflect your main point. For instance, if you are writing a review, the title should refer to the item being reviewed without giving away details about the film, book, or show. The title should serve as an invitation to read the piece or attend the performance because it contains just enough information to lure the reader by making him or her curious. For opinion pieces, an exclamatory title helps catch a reader's attention. Keep it short and to the point. Rhetorical questions can also work to draw in an audience. If you've written a persuasive letter, no title is necessary. However, you do need to make sure that you have a heading that includes the correct address and names, and that you've added the date.

Once a title is chosen, examine your writing for spelling and punctuation errors. If you've typed your piece on a computer, now is a good time to use the spell-check function.

KEY

✔ **Add an informative title that illustrates your main point.**

✔ **Complete a spelling and grammar check.**

✔ **Get feedback from others.**

For handwritten stories, use your dictionary to look up words that don't seem correct. At this stage you probably feel like you know the piece well, but pretend you are reading it for the first time. This will help you to catch places where grammar, spelling, or clarity need to be improved. Often, your computer's spell-check function will catch grammatical mistakes, but you also need to be on the lookout for clunky sentences, missed commas, improper punctuation, or any other errors.

Verb Agreement

So that the effect of your persuasive argument is fully felt, make sure that any confusion in the writing is clarified. Verb tense agreement is important, so in this final proofreading stage, examine your verbs very carefully. Make sure that tenses match from the beginning to the end of your piece (see examples, page 35). If your persuasive writing has to do with a current situation, then it needs to be written in the present tense. If you are referring to something that has happened before, use the past tense; and if you're focusing on an issue yet to happen, then the future tense is the way to go.

The Whole Package

To ensure that your piece has the correct focus and sets the proper tone to be thoroughly convincing, set it aside for a day and then reread it with "fresh" eyes. Another idea is to join a partner for a final read-through. Have your partner read your story to reexamine its basic elements. Use the following list to refresh your memory.

Sentence Types
- Can short sentences be combined to make them more interesting?
- Should longer sentences be divided into two more powerful and precise thoughts?

Consider adding a rhetorical question or exclamation to add impact.

Paragraph Structure
- Are the transitions from paragraph to paragraph smooth?
- Does each paragraph focus on one specific point?
- Do all the sentences in the paragraph support the main point?
- Do the sentences flow in a logical order?

ASK YOURSELF

☐ Will my title persuade someone to read my piece?

☐ Have the spelling and grammar been checked?

☐ Have I made editing changes to polish the final version of my persuasive piece?

Finding an Editor

An editor is someone who can help you shape your writing. He or she will offer suggestions and point out areas that need improvement. Especially with persuasive pieces, the full impact of your writing can only be felt if it is seen by others. When revising your final document, you should avoid a total rewrite. You should instead focus on specific areas that need improvement. This is where an editor or a writing partner will come in handy.

When choosing an editor, it is best to not depend on someone who knows you too well. In that case, he or she probably thinks that everything you do is wonderful or may be nervous about hurting your feelings. The point isn't that your feelings are hurt, but instead that your partner is not afraid to ask you questions about what might not be clear in your writing. You want to depend on his or her ability to be persuaded by the information.

There are many ways that you can work with an editor to improve your writing. While he or she reads the piece, watch his or her facial expressions. Ask questions about his or her reaction. Get out your notes and correct any rough patches. Another angle is to read your piece during an informal gathering to get a group's reaction. Hand out a sheet with some questions pertaining to the piece, and have your listeners fill out

Types of Verb Tense

Example of Present Tense:
I feel that the food in the cafeteria needs to be much better. *I know* that this could happen easily if school officials agreed to sit down and discuss our menu choices.

Example of Past Tense:
I remember that the food in the cafeteria *was* so much better last year when the school had International Day every Friday and the students *tried* different foods.

Example of Future Tense:
The food in the cafeteria *will improve* if school officials take some time to determine what students like to eat and what is healthy for them.

your survey after you've finished. Tell them they don't need to put their names on it, but only answer the questions honestly.

Example Questionnaire

- List three reasons why this piece was convincing.

- Which statement stood out the most?

- Was any information unclear, and therefore wasn't persuasive?

When you enlist the help of another person, your piece will be that much better for it. If you find that you don't have a chance to go through this process with someone else, find a tape recorder and read your persuasive story into it. Play it back and listen to how it sounds. Listen for any clumsy sentences so that you can correct them. Example of an edited draft:

"Good Taste"
It is my opinion that the food in the cafeteria of Millerbrook School could be improved through better food choices. The options offered now by the cafeteria are boring. Just as students are encouraged to investigate different world cultures, so too does an understanding of foods found in those cultures become important.
While I know that not everyone may like the idea of changing school lunches to include cuisine that they've never heard of, I think that it would be enlightening. I'm not suggesting that the cafeteria entirely do away with standard fare, but why not

add more variety? Along with the daily choices, include an Indian curry dish or Mexican enchiladas.

I have talked with students from other schools who are offered a variety of food choices, so I know that it's possible. I also know that kosher and vegetarian food is available in our cafeteria for some students, but why isn't it available for everyone?

You might be asking, "But how will the cooks ever find those recipes?" Well, here is my answer: hold a contest! In the school newsletter, there could be an invitation to submit favorite family recipes. This way, Millerbrook students would have a chance to try foods from many lands. I feel that this would be a great learning experience.

Proofreading Symbols

When you or someone else is correcting your piece, here are the symbols that should be used to give instructions for corrections:

insert a comma	delete	a space needed here
apostrophe or single quotation mark	transpose elements	begin new paragraph
insert something	close up this space	no paragraph
use double quotation marks	use a period here	

Presentation

Now that you've created your persuasive piece, you want to make sure that your final version is presented in a way that will be effective.

The words and meaning of a persuasive piece are important, but the form in which it is presented will also have an impact on your reader's interest. The way in which writing is presented has a huge impact on how we respond to it. If you think of almost any product, you'll notice that its packaging makes it more attractive. In writing presentations, this theory also holds true. Since a persuasive piece depends on its audience to exist, make sure that it is as inviting to look at as it is convincing to read.

First, start with the words. If they are typed, make sure the font and size are easily readable and the ink color is standard blue or black. That holds true for handwritten pieces as well. The neatness of your type and the color of the ink

KEY

✔ **Put together final draft.**

✔ **Fine-tune it for presentation.**

✔ **Look for interesting places to present the piece.**

both need to be straightforward, unless you've been instructed otherwise. Next, think about the form of your persuasive piece.

For a letter, the standard letter format must be used with the date at the top and the correct salutation and address. If you have any questions about these facts, do a little research and make sure you've got it correct, because you'll have a hard time convincing someone if you've misspelled his or her name or sent the letter to the wrong address.

Regarding a review, you might want to use graphics or photographs to enhance the piece. This kind of additional attention can really bring your point to life, especially if you are persuading the reader to take part in whatever activity you're reviewing. There is nothing more convincing than a picture to make a person visualize a point of view. If you use a picture that someone else has taken, remember to give that person credit.

If you've written an opinion piece that would best fit into a newspaper, you can print the story in columns. But check first with your teacher to make sure of the format he or she requested. Opinion pieces usually stand on their own without any additional graphics because the words carry the whole story.

Last and certainly not least, you must make sure that your name is featured on your story. This is important so that readers can appreciate whose opinion they're reading.

Places to Persuade

Since the style of persuasive writing is so dependent on the outside world for a response, there are quite a few options for how to present your work. Here are some ideas:

- Get a letter-writing campaign together about an important issue in your school or community. Gather some persuasive letters and send them to the source, then see what impact they have. There is always power in numbers, and if your persuasive letters are well presented with a clear message, you can end up making an impression. At the very least, you should receive a reply back as to why the idea is a good one or not.

- Talk to your peers, classmates, or teachers about a cause that you feel strongly about. If there are others who feel the same way, consider holding a rally to present your views. Write persuasive speeches (opinion pieces), hang banners with catchy persuasive slogans (sayings with impact), or invite a person from outside (by writing a persuasive letter) who also holds your point of view to be a guest speaker.

- Find a local or school paper where you can submit an opinion piece about something you feel strongly about.

- Write a persuasive letter to a magazine, newspaper, or television station about something you've seen in its pages or on its network. Explain why you agreed or disagreed with what you saw.

- As you can tell, there are many reasons to learn to write an effectively persuasive article, letter, review, or opinionated editorial. If you practice backing up your opinions with appropriate facts, then persuasive writing will eventually come naturally.

Plenty of magazines publish many different forms of student writing on the Internet. For persuasive pieces, you can find many forums where you might offer your opinions. A good place to research what's out there is www.stonesoup.com where there are links to magazines and other outlets for student writing. Other opportunities to see your writing online and in print are located in the back of this book.

Glossary

anecdote A short, entertaining account of an event.

argue To give reasons for or against something.

complex sentence A sentence formed by one independent clause and one or more dependent clauses.

compound sentence A sentence in which two independent clauses are joined together with a coordinate conjunction.

conjunction A word used to connect individual words or groups of words.

credit Acknowledgment of work done.

declarative sentence A sentence that makes a strong statement.

dependent clause A clause that cannot stand on its own and depends on the rest of a sentence to make sense.

editor Someone who prepares writing for presentation.

essay A piece of writing in which a single topic is presented, explained, and described in an interesting way.

first draft The first writing of a piece without worrying about mistakes.

format The style or manner of a piece of writing.

grammar The guidelines and rules followed in order to speak and write acceptably.

graphic A picture, graph, or map used to illustrate a piece.

graphic organizer Something used to gather and organize thoughts and details for writing.

hyperbole Figurative language that uses extreme exaggeration.

independent clause A clause that expresses a complete thought and can stand alone as a sentence.

Internet Short for "interconnected networks." A place to search for information from sources all over the world.

metaphor A figure of speech that compares two things that are not alike to each other without using "like" or "as."

objective Being without bias or prejudice.

opinion A belief based on feelings.

outline A general plan.

paragraph A group of sentences all relating to one subject.

paraphrase To reword something spoken or printed.

personification Using figurative language to give something that is not human lifelike qualities.

perspective A specific point of view when investigating something.

phrase A group of related words that do not express complete thoughts.

plagiarism Taking someone else's writing and passing it off as one's own.

point of view Perspective; opinion.

proofreading Checking the final copy for any errors.

punctuation Marks used in writing to support the piece.

report Account given or opinion expressed about a particular topic.

research Careful study and investigation into a topic.

review A critical evaluation of a book, movie, and so on.

revise To review your writing.

simile A figure of speech that compares two things that are not alike by using "like" or "as."

source The place where information is provided.

subject The topic of a writing piece.

subjective Resulting from the feeling of a person; personal.

theory The analysis of a set of facts in their relation to one another.

thesaurus A book similar to a dictionary that offers synonyms.

title The heading of a piece of writing.

topic The subject of a piece of writing.

topic sentence A sentence that describes what the piece of writing will be about.

transition Tying two ideas together smoothly with a word or phrase.

verb A word that shows action or links the subject to another word in the sentence.

For More Information

National Council of Teachers of English (NCTE)
Achievement Awards in Writing
1111 Kenyon Road
Urbana, IL 61901-1096
Web site: http://www.ncte.org

National Scholastic Press Association (NSPA)
2221 University Avenue SE, Suite 121
Minneapolis, MN 55414
Web site: http://www.studentpress.org

Reading, Writing, and Art Awards
Weekly Reader Corporation
200 First Stamford Place
P.O. Box 120023
Stamford, CT 06912-0023
Web site: http://
   www.weeklyreader.com

The Scholastic Art and Writing Awards
555 Broadway
New York, NY 10012
Web site: http://www.scholastic.com

Web Sites

Due to the changing nature of Internet links, the Rosen Publishing Group, Inc., has developed an online list of Web sites related to the subject of this book. This site is updated regularly. Please use this link to access the list:

http://www.rosenlinks.com/lws/pewri

Getting Published

Merlyn's Pen
Fiction, Essays, and Poems by
   America's Teens
P.O. Box 910
East Greenwich, RI 02818
Web site: http://www.merlynspen.com

Skipping Stones
Multicultural Children's Magazine
P.O. Box 3939
Eugene, OR 97403
Web site: http://
   www.skippingstones.org

Stone Soup
The Magazine by Young Writers
   and Artists
P.O. Box 83

Santa Cruz, CA 95063
Web site: http://www.stonesoup.com

TeenInk
P.O. Box 30
Newton, MA 02161
Web site: http://www.teenink.com
Teen Voices
P.O. Box 120-027
Boston, MA 02112
Web site: http://www.teenvoices.com

Young Voices Magazine
P.O. Box 2321
Olympia, WA 98507
Web site: http://
   youngvoicesmagazine.com

For Further Reading

Culham, Ruth. *6+1 Traits of Writing: The Complete Guide*. New York: Scholastic, 2003.

Fletcher, Ralph. *A Writer's Notebook: Unlocking the Writer Within You*. New York: HarperTrophy, 2003.

Sebranek, Patrick. *Writers Inc.: A Student Handbook for Writing and Learning.* Wilmington, MA: Great Source Educational Group, Inc., 2000.

Zaragoza, Nina. *Rethinking Language Arts: Passion and Practice* (Teaching and Thinking). New York: Routledge, 2002.

Bibliography

Ace Writing. "The Writing Process." 2002. Retrieved July 7, 2003 (http://www.geocities.com/fifth_grade_tpes/index.html).

Creative Writing for Teens. "How to Format a Manuscript for Publication." 2003. Retrieved June 20, 2003 (http://www.teenwriting.about.com/cs/formatting/ht/FormatManu.htm).

Creative Writing for Teens. "Tips on Writing from the Creative Writing for Teens Community." 2003. Retrieved August 26, 2003 (http://www.teenwriting.about.com/library/submissions/bltipssub.htm).

English Biz. "Writing to Describe and Original Writing." 2003. Retrieved October 16, 2003 (http://www.englishbiz.co.uk/mainguides/describe.htm).

Feder, Barnaby J. "With the Apples Arriving by E-Mail, Teachers Adapt." *New York Times*, August 14, 2003, p. G5.

Guernsey, Lisa. "A Young Writer's Roundtable, via the Web." *New York Times*, August 14, 2003, p. G1.

"Guide to Grammar and Writing." 2003. Retrieved August 1, 2003 (http://webster.commnet.edu/grammar/index.htm).

Hewitt, John. "Fifteen Craft Exercises for Writers." Writers Resource Center Online. Retrieved June 25, 2003 (http://www.poewar.com/articles/15_exercises.htm).

Kemper, Dave, Patrick Sebranek, and Verne Meyer. *All Write: A Student Handbook for Writing and Learning.* Wilmington, MA: Great Source Education Group, 1998.

LEO: Literacy Education Online. "The Write Place Catalogue." 1997. Retrieved July 10, 2003 (http://leo.stcloudstate.edu/acadwrite/descriptive.html).

Scholastic for Teachers. "Writing with Writers." 2003. Retrieved June 20, 2003 (http://teacher.scholastic.com/writewit/).

Stone Soup. "Links for Young Writers." 2004. Retrieved June 20, 2003 (http://www.stonesoup.com/main2/links.html).

Teacher Created Materials. "Language Arts." 2000. Retrieved July 21, 2003 (http://www.teachercreated.com).

Winthrop, Elizabeth. "Some Practical Advice on Writing and Publishing for Young Writers." 1998. Retrieved August 26, 2003 (http://www.elizabethwinthrop.com/advice.html).

Index

About the Author

Lauren Spencer is originally from California and now lives in New York City, where she teaches writing workshops in public schools. She also writes lifestyle and music articles for magazines.

Credits

Designer: Geri Fletcher; **Editor:** Joann Jovinelly